T0417660

FANtastic Franchises

BARBIE FRANCHISE

Kenny Abdo

Fly!
An Imprint of Abdo Zoom
abdobooks.com

abdobooks.com

Published by Abdo Zoom, a division of ABDO, P.O. Box 398166, Minneapolis, Minnesota 55439.

Printed in the United States of America, North Mankato, Minnesota.
052024
092024

Photo Credits: Alamy, AP Images, Everett Collection, Getty Images, Shutterstock, ©UCLA p6 / CC BY 4.0
Production Contributors: Kenny Abdo, Jennie Forsberg, Grace Hansen
Design Contributors: Candice Keimig, Neil Klinepier, Colleen McLaren

Library of Congress Control Number: 2023948526

Publisher's Cataloging-in-Publication Data

Names: Abdo, Kenny, author.
Title: Barbie franchise / by Kenny Abdo
Description: Minneapolis, Minnesota : Abdo Zoom, 2025 | Series: FANtastic franchises | Includes online resources and index.
Identifiers: ISBN 9781098285562 (lib. bdg.) | ISBN 9781098286262 (ebook) | ISBN 9781098286613 (Read-to-me eBook)
Subjects: LCSH: Mattel, Inc. Barbie Doll Division--Juvenile literature. | Barbie (Fictitious character)--Juvenile literature. | Barbie dolls--Juvenile literature. | Dolls--Juvenile literature. | Branding (Marketing)--Juvenile literature. | Popular culture--Juvenile literature.
Classification: DDC 338.768--dc23

TABLE OF CONTENTS

Barbie.......................... 4

Origins 6

Through the Years.............. 10

Fandom 20

Glossary 22

Online Resources 23

Index 24

For more than 60 years, Barbara Millicent Roberts has been the most popular fashion doll on the market. But she's known better as Barbie!

jest
Chelsea
Barbie
Chelsea
Barbie
EXTRA MINIS
34.99
34.99
39.99
79.99
Barbie
29.99
29.99

ORIGINS

One day, Ruth Handler watched her daughter play with baby dolls. Handler was the co-founder of Mattel. She saw that there was a need for toys that young girls would look up to. So, Handler decided to create them!

Handler was inspired by the glamorous stars of the 1950s. She named the new doll after her daughter, Barbara. In 1959, the first Barbie doll was introduced to the world!

THROUGH THE YEARS

In the first year, more than 300,000 Barbie dolls were sold. The first Barbie sold for just $3.00. Today, an original Barbie in **mint condition** can sell for $25,000!

Barbie bought her first Dreamhouse in 1962. It was made entirely out of cardboard. The Dreamhouse had a plastic upgrade shortly after. It has been **renovated** through the years to reflect the time.

Over the years, Barbie has had more than 250 careers. She even went to space in 1965! Since then, Barbie has been everything from a doctor to a rock star!

BARBIE
FIRE RESCUE
Firefighter
1995

The first official Black and Latina Barbies were released in 1980. That same year saw the first of more than 40 different international Barbies released to date.

In 2016, Mattel introduced Barbie Fashionistas. Those dolls came in different body types, skin tones, and hairstyles. They accurately reflected the **diversity** of modern women.

Barbie joined Buzz, Woody, and friends in *Toy Story 2* in 1999. She has appeared in every movie of the series since.

In 2001, Mattel began producing **CGI** animated films based on Barbie. There have been several movies and many TV shows following Barbie and her adventures!

The **live-action** *Barbie* film was released in 2023. The hilarious and heartfelt movie was the first female-directed film to **gross** $1 billion. It was also nominated for best picture at the 2024 **Academy Awards**!

FANDOM

Fans of Barbie can experience her in many ways. There have been apps, social media accounts, and book series created for Barbie. There have also been fashion shows dedicated to the plastic **icon**!

More than one billion Barbie dolls have been sold worldwide. In fact, a Barbie doll is sold every three seconds. At 11-inches tall, Barbie towers over everything else!

GLOSSARY

Academy Award – a ceremony held annually to present awards that recognize achievement in the film industry.

CGI – short for computer-generated imagery, the creation of still or animated visual content using imaging software.

diversity – the state of being all different kinds or sorts.

gross – total.

icon – a person or thing that people recognize as a symbol of something and is an object of great respect and admiration.

live-action – involving real, traditional actors and cameras.

mint condition – new or as if new.

renovate – to upgrade a space or house by rebuilding or repairing.

ONLINE RESOURCES

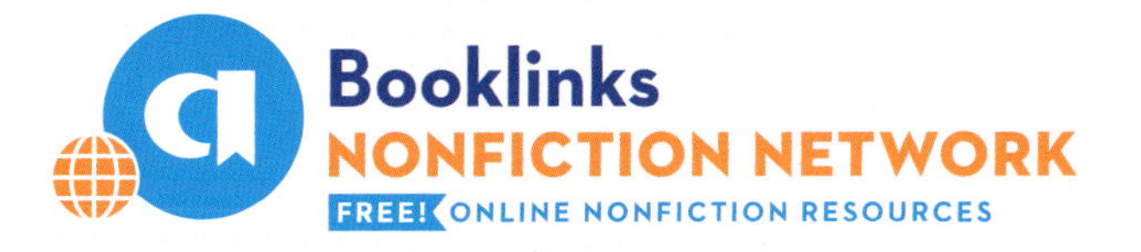

To learn more about the Barbie franchise, please visit **abdobooklinks.com** or scan this QR code. These links are routinely monitored and updated to provide the most current information available.

INDEX

Academy Awards 18

Barbie (character) 4, 11, 12, 16, 17

Barbie (movie) 18

Barbie (toy) 8, 10, 14, 15, 21

Dreamhouse (toy) 11

fans 20

Handler, Ruth 7, 8

Mattel (company) 7, 15, 17

Toy Story 2 (movie) 16

TV series 17